Christmas in the American Southwest

CHRISTMAS IN THE
AMERICAN SOUTHWEST

Christmas Around the World
From World Book

World Book, Inc.
a Scott Fetzer company

CHICAGO   LONDON   SYDNEY   TORONTO

STAFF

Publisher Emeritus
William H. Nault

President
John Frere

Vice President, Editor in Chief
Dick Dell

Vice President and Editorial
Director, Product Development
Michael Ross

EDITORIAL

Managing Editor
Maureen Mostyn Liebenson

Associate Editor
Karen Zack Ingebretsen

Writer
Ellen Hughes

Permissions Editor
Janet T. Peterson

ART

Executive Director
Roberta Dimmer

Art Director
Wilma Stevens

Senior Designer
Brenda B. Tropinski

Senior Photographs Editor
Sandra Dyrlund

Photographs Editor
Kelly Mountain

PRODUCT PRODUCTION

Vice President, Production and Technology
Daniel N. Bach

Director of Manufacturing/Pre-Press
Sandra Van den Broucke

Manufacturing Manager
Barbara Podczerwinski

Senior Production Manager
Randi Park

Proofreaders
Anne Dillon
Karen Lenburg

DIRECT MARKETING

Director, Product Development
Paul Kobasa

World Book wishes to thank the following individuals for their contributions to CHRISTMAS IN THE AMERICAN SOUTHWEST: Nancy Harbert, Kathy Hazelbaker, Debra Porter, Katie Sharp, and Steele Communications.

Cover Credits; Tom Bean, DRK; Randall Roberts; David Stoecklei, AdStock Photos

```
Library of Congress Cataloging-in-Publication Data
Christmas in the American Southwest.
     p.  cm. -- (Christmas around the world from World Book)
   Summary: Surveys of the Christmas traditions celebrated in New
Mexico, Texas, Arizona, and Oklahoma. Includes carols, recipes, and
crafts.
   ISBN 0-7166-0896-0    ISBN 0-7166-0857-X (trade)
   1. Christmas--Southwest, New--Juvenile literature. 2. Southwest,
New--Social life and customs--Juvenile literature. [1. Christmas-
-Southwest, New. 2. Southwest, New--Social life and customs.]
I. Series.
GT 4986.S64C57  1996
394.2'663'0979--dc20                                    96-8416
```

© 1996 World Book, Inc. All rights reserved. This volume may not be reproduced in whole or in part in any form without prior written permission from the publisher.

World Book, Inc.
525 W. Monroe
Chicago, IL 60661

Printed in Singapore
3 4 5 6 7 8 9 10 01 00 99 98 97 96

CONTENTS

Introduction 6

Spanish and Native American
Traditions 8

Southwest Christmas Past 20

Cowboy Christmas 34

Lighting the Western Sky 40

Big City and Small Town
Celebrations 48

All the Trimmings 58

Southwest Crafts 65

Southwest Carols 74

Southwest Recipes 76

Farolitos, or little fires nestled inside small paper bags, are a common sight at Christmastime in the Southwest. Here, the little lanterns illuminate the interior of the Tumacacori Mission on Christmas Eve. The mission, located near Tubac, Arizona, was opened in 1822.

Introduction

Christmas arrived early in the American Southwest. Long before there was a Plymouth, Massachusetts, or a Jamestown, Virginia, hundreds of years before the first wagon trains rolled west, some present-day Christmas traditions were thriving in the wide-open spaces that today are known as the states of Arizona, New Mexico, Texas, and Oklahoma.

Ancestors of the region's many Native American peoples had inhabited this land for thousands of years when Coronado and his army of conquistadors marched north from Mexico in 1540. In his wake came Spanish padres who set about building missions and converting the native people to Christianity. Before long, a joyful mingling of Spanish and Indian customs defined Christmas in the Southwest.

Then came groups of settlers from back East and from Europe. They, too, brought Christmas traditions to share and discovered new meaning in the traditions found here.

Finally, the wide-open and wildly beautiful land itself has helped shape the rich and deeply spiritual celebration of Christmas in the American Southwest.

Many cultures come together in the Southwest. Native American customs, such as the Buffalo Dance shown here, have had a strong influence on the region's celebration of Christmas.

The American Southwest spreads out over a vast area that is sometimes referred to as the "wide-open spaces." The region includes the states of Oklahoma, Texas, Arizona, and New Mexico.

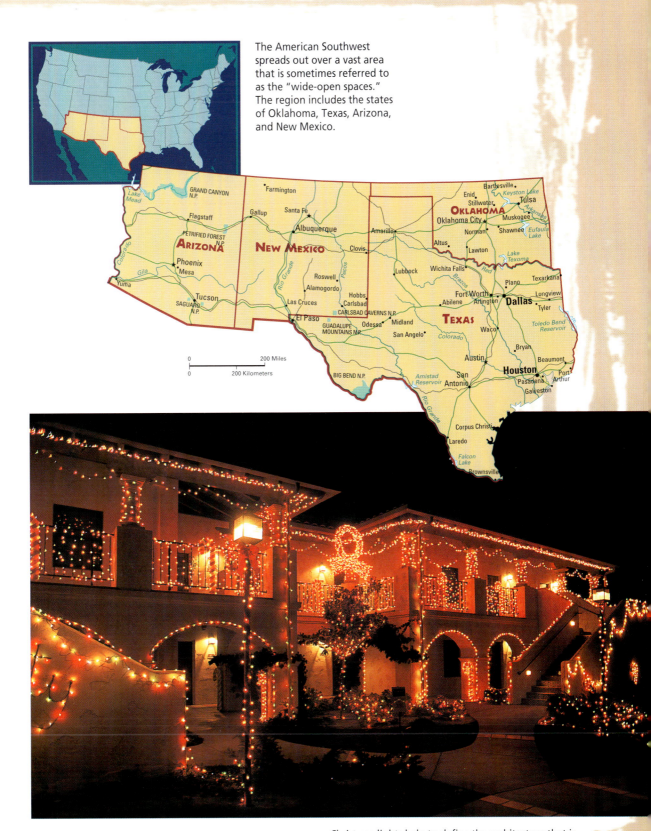

Christmas lights help to define the architecture that is characteristic of the American Southwest, which blends the styles of ancient and modern times.

Spanish and Native American Traditions

It looks like Christmas here in the American Southwest; like Christmas of another time, that is. In the pueblos of New Mexico and the small towns of Arizona, low adobe and wooden houses, ancient mission churches, and the surrounding desert landscape all take the spirit back to an ancient time.

Upon a second look, present-day signs of Christmas are also quite prevalent. Wreaths and hanging *ristras* (18- to 60-inch-long bunches of bright red chile peppers) adorn the thick, worn wooden doors. Playful electric strings of chile-pepper lights trim a window here and there. Children line *farolitos*, or "little lanterns," along the walkways that lead to their homes.

As Christmas approaches, groups of friends walk the streets of town seeking shelter for "Mary" and

All dressed up in winter white, these buildings of Taos Pueblo, New Mexico, nearly 100 miles north of Santa Fe, stand ready to shelter those celebrating the unique traditions of Christmas in the American Southwest.

"Joseph." Others climb a mountain to pray. Dancers in richly decorated traditional costumes prepare for a ceremonial Christmas Eve dance at the bonfire in front of a mission church.

In the 1500's, the first Spanish missionaries arrived in the Southwest. Led by a powerful faith, these few religious men built missions throughout New Mexico, Arizona, and Texas and brought the story of Christmas alive for the Native Americans living there. Joined in faith, the Spanish missionaries and their Indian converts combined centuries of tradition from two separate cultures into a rich celebration unique to the American Southwest.

Fiesta of Our Lady of Guadalupe

The celebration of Christmas for Hispanic and many Native American Southwesterners begins each year with the Fiesta of Our Lady of Guadalupe on December 12. The religious festival commemorates the appearance of the Virgin Mary to Juan Diego, an Indian in Mexico in 1531.

This vision of Mary spoke to the newly converted man and left an impression of her face on his *tilma,* a robe of woven cactus fiber. Our Lady of Guadalupe, as the vision was named, is considered the patron saint of the Americas. She is the saint who aids believers in their daily lives, lightening their burdens and protecting their homes. Because the first appearance of Our Lady of Guadalupe in the new world marked the real acceptance of Christianity by the native peoples, celebration of the event is a fitting start for Christmas.

In villages throughout the Southwest, the Fiesta of Our Lady of Guadalupe is celebrated with *Los Matachines,* a traditional Spanish folk dance. Masked dancers dressed in colorful costumes adorned with bells, feathers, and other decorations are accompanied by musicians playing violins, guitars, drums, and accordions. The ensemble makes its way toward the town church, following a statue of the community's patron saint.

Possibly the most dramatic celebration of the Fiesta of Our Lady of Guadalupe is held in Tortugas, a small village near the southern border of New Mexico. Here the celebration is enlivened with the customs of the Tiwa Indians, whose ancestors settled in the area. The three-day celebration begins as up to two dozen *danzantes,* or dancers, dressed in feathered headdresses and colorful clothing perform

The small village of Tortugas, New Mexico, is home to a dramatic celebration of the Fiesta of Our Lady of Guadalupe. As part of the celebration, parishioners gather before an image of the Virgin for an all-night prayer vigil.

traditional Tiwa steps before a small statue of the Virgin. At the Casa del Pueblo, a small community hall where the image of Our Lady of Guadalupe had been carried in a candlelight procession, several hundred more people gather for an all-night prayer vigil.

Throughout the next day, more than 700 people make the two-hour, five-mile pilgrimage from the town to the top of nearby Tortugas Mountain. Carrying torches to light their way, the townspeople are joined by people who come from miles away to participate in this religious experience. As they near the top, celebrants gather wood for a fire. High atop the mountain, they join in a Mass celebrated by the local bishop of the Roman Catholic church. They then spend hours singing, praying, and reciting the rosary before returning to the village.

After the dance and the pilgrimage to the mountaintop, all are welcome to a feast prepared by a number of local cooks. Traditional foods include *albondigas* (meatballs) cooked in beef broth; red chile with meat; beans; and Indian bread.

Las Posadas

Las Posadas, "the inns," is a much-loved Christmas tradition introduced to the Southwest more than 400 years ago. The custom is credited to Fray Diego de Soria, an Augustinian missionary who expanded a traditional *novena* (a prayer said on nine successive days) to recall the journey of Mary and Joseph into a full reenactment.

Traditionally, Las Posadas begins on December 16. For nine nights worshipers carry carved figures of Mary and Joseph as they travel through the village streets asking for shelter. At each home, the travelers sing traditional songs and repeat their request. Turned away again and again, they finally hear *"Entren santos peregrinos,"* ("Enter holy pilgrims") and are admitted to a home. The *Misterios,* carved folk images of Joseph and Mary, are placed in a specially prepared altar in the home. Plenty of food and drink and a piñata party for the children follow.

Elaborate artwork graces the walls and ceilings of San Xavier Mission in Tucson, Arizona, where parishioners celebrate at Christmastime and throughout the year.

Though today it is generally reduced to a one-night pageant on Christmas Eve or the night before, Las Posadas remains essential to Christmas in the Southwest. The traditional songs accompanied by guitar and the conversation between Joseph and the innkeeper are the same whether shared in a little pageant by neighbors or performed as a citywide celebration.

Full nine-night Las Posadas observances are sponsored by several Catholic churches in Albuquerque, New Mexico. Parishioners gather at Holy Rosary Church, Holy Family Church, or Our Lady of Sorrows Church each night to travel to different houses, joining in song, prayer, food, and celebration. On Christmas Eve each "journey" ends at the church itself.

In Santa Fe, Las Posadas is acted out in one night on the city's historic plaza. Afterward, the crowd enters the nearby courtyard of the Palace of the Governors for hot chocolate and *bizcochitos,* traditional Christmas sugar cookies with anise.

At La Puerta de Oro ("The Golden Door") Senior Center in Oklahoma City, a reenactment of Las Posadas takes place indoors. Doors around the center are decorated to look like different inns. Participants travel from door to door requesting shelter for "Mary." Once "Mary" and "Joseph" are accepted, hot chocolate and pastries are served, and children from the community enjoy a piñata party.

Throughout the Southwest, homes make room for Mary and Joseph on one special night. Often holiday food and drink are served at every stop, and the members of each house join the procession as it passes. Carols are sung around the family's *nacimiento* (nativity scene), and hot chocolate and bizcochitos are served.

For more than 30 years, the San Antonio Conservation Society has staged a beautiful reenactment of Las Posadas along San Antonio's River Walk. Here thousands of city residents, choirs, tourists, and mariachis join "Mary" and "Joseph" as they travel from inn to inn, seeking shelter. The candlelit procession begins in the early evening at the Mansion del Rio hotel, and winds its way along the gaily decorated River Walk. The journey is lit by thousands of glowing *luminarias,* or small bonfires. Singing traditional Posadas songs and Christmas carols, the travelers make their way to the Arneson River Theater. Here the Holy Family finds a humble stable for shelter. There is song and celebration, followed by a piñata party for the children at nearby Maverick Plaza.

Las Posadas

(English translation)

Saint Joseph: Who will give lodging to these pilgrims, who are tired out from traveling the highways?

Innkeeper: However much you may say that you are worn out, we do not give lodging to strangers.

Saint Joseph: In the name of heaven, I beg of you lodging, since my beloved wife can travel no longer.

Innkeeper: There is no lodging here; keep on moving. I cannot open to you, don't be stupid.

Saint Joseph: Don't be inhuman and have pity, for the God of the Heavens will reward you for it.

Innkeeper: Now you may go away and not bother me, because if I get mad I'm going to beat you.

Saint Joseph: We come worn out from Nazareth; I am a carpenter by the name of Joseph.

Innkeeper: Your name doesn't concern me; let me sleep, since I have already told you that we are not to open to you.

Saint Joseph: Lodging, dear Innkeeper, for only one night, the Queen of the Heavens begs of you.

Innkeeper: Well then if she is a queen who asks it, how is it that at night she goes so unattended?

Saint Joseph: My wife is Mary, the Queen of the Heavens; mother she will be of the Divine Word.

Innkeeper: Is it you, Joseph and your wife Mary? Enter, pilgrims; I did not know you.

Saint Joseph: Happy be this house that gives us lodging; may God always give you your sacred happiness.

Innkeeper: Lodging we give you with much happiness; enter, honest Joseph, enter with Mary.

Chorus (from without): Enter saintly pilgrims; receive this ovation, not from this poor dwelling, but from my heart.

Chorus (from within): This night is (made) of happiness, of pleasure, and of rejoicing, because we give lodging here to the Mother of the Son of God.

For more than 30 years, Los Pastores del Valle de Mesilla has been performing the medieval folk play in churches across New Mexico, Arizona, and Texas.

On each December weekend before Christmas, San Antonio's *Fiestas Navideñas* celebration fills the nearby Market Square with Spanish-flavored holiday fun. There are piñata parties, tamale-making contests, and plenty of *buñuelos* (crispy, sugar-coated tortillas). Pancho Claus, Santa's black-bearded cousin from the South Pole, arrives wearing a charro hat and red poncho. Created by a local serviceman more than 15 years ago, Pancho Claus presents toys and food to needy families at Christmas.

Los Pastores

A medieval religious folk play used by Spanish missionaries to bring the Christmas story to life for their Native American congregations is working its holiday magic again in cities throughout the Southwest.

Unlike the sweet and gentle Las Posadas procession, *Los Pastores* (The Shepherds) offers a rollicking, often hilarious, somewhat shocking recounting of the misadventures of the shepherds on their way to see the newborn Christ Child.

Along with the Holy Family and the usual shepherds and angels, the cast of characters for Los Pastores includes a determined Lucifer and his child-sized assistants; a hapless, drunken shepherd named Bartolo; Bartolo's wife; and an old hermit. Costumes place the shepherds squarely in the Southwest, with serapes, sandals, and sombreros. The plot loosely follows the errant shepherd Bartolo's wayward course to his sudden redemption kneeling before the Christ Child, taking many hilarious and surprising stops along the way.

Los Pastores del Valle de Mesilla, a group organized by a Franciscan priest at a retreat near Las Cruces, New Mexico, has been performing the folk play for more than 30 years to audiences in churches across New Mexico, Texas, and Arizona. The 50-member cast includes a father and daughter portraying Joseph and Mary, and three generations of a single family on stage together.

Rather than fading with changing times, Los Pastores and other religious folk-play performances are attracting more enthusiastic audiences each year. With its central struggle between good and evil, its wild and clever characters, its songs and good humor, Los Pastores is an irresistible piece of Christmas magic.

A SWINGING-GOOD CHRISTMAS

The piñata, a Mexican tradition that adds fun to birthdays and celebrations throughout the year, is a natural part of the Christmas celebration for children of the American Southwest.

Containers made of earthenware or papier-mâché, piñatas come in many shapes, sizes, and colors. With a hollow core, they are stuffed with candy, fruits, and toys—but not for long. When the party begins, the piñata is hung above the heads of the eager youngsters. Then the children are blindfolded and take turns trying to break the piñata with a stick. The adults have their fun by pulling on the rope that holds the piñata, thus whisking it out of reach. But inevitably one child will break the piñata, and the children scramble for their just rewards.

Tamales—cornmeal and ground meat wrapped in cornhusks—are popular fare for the celebration of Las Posadas and are enjoyed throughout the year.

Little Fires

*The little fires that blaze on
  Christmas Eve
Are lit by simple folks whose
  hearts believe
The Christ Child wanders softly
  through the night
And blesses all who set a
  guiding light.
(O Little Child, I tend my fire
  and pray
For fires around the world
  to guide Thy way.)*

—Dorothy Linney
* *New Mexico Magazine, December 1935.
Reprinted with permission.*

Farolitos light up the Southwest Christmas season in Old Town Albuquerque. These little lanterns cast a warm glow outside homes, community buildings, and businesses across the region.

In their celebrations of Christmas in the 1500's, the native peoples of the Southwest built bonfires of twigs and branches in front of churches and pueblos. These fires lit the way to Mass and, symbolically, lit the way for Mary and Joseph in their search for shelter.

Were these early bonfires—the first luminarias—the cultural descendents of the fires shepherds set long ago on the hillsides of Spain to warm themselves on winter nights? Were the first luminarias derived from an ancient ceremonial custom of the Native American peoples? Both theories, both cultures, join in the annual lighting of the traditional Christmas Eve bonfires. Each year, as they illuminate the way for the Christ Child, glowing luminarias stand on pueblo squares and before churches and homes as a symbol of the natural blending of cultures in the celebration of Christmas in the American Southwest.

Traditional luminarias are constructed of fragrant piñon pine logs, crisscrossed and stacked in a square three feet high. Once a common Christmas Eve sight on any street in New Mexico, luminarias have become more rare as cities have become more crowded. Still, in the pueblos and some of the smaller towns and villages of northern New Mexico, the tradition of lighting luminarias continues unabated. In Albuquerque, buses take sightseers on a luminaria tour of the city's Old Town, Country Club, and Los Altos neighborhoods, where the displays are legendary.

Though the bonfires are fewer, the welcoming path for the Christ Child glows brightly as people line walkways, windows, and roofs everywhere with *farolitos.* Also called luminarias, farolitos (from the Spanish for "little torch") are lighted candles set inside small paper bags and placed in rows outside on Christmas Eve. Each 12-inch bag is cuffed around the top, filled with several inches of sand, and put in its place before a votive candle is pushed into the sand and lighted. Displays wind down walkways, over roofs, and all around courtyards.

The first farolitos were Chinese paper lanterns. When they became available in the Southwest in the early 1800's, people gingerly placed the colorful, delicate lights along walls and walkways, adapting the Spanish tradition of stringing festival lights in celebration.

By the 1820's, all kinds of useful goods were arriving over the Santa Fe Trail, including plain brown wrapping paper. Christmas celebrants soon discovered that farolitos made with simple, sturdy, little brown paper bags created a warm glow against adobe walls that no fancy lantern could match. Today the glowing brown bags remain the symbol of the Southwest at Christmas.

Are they farolitos or luminarias? To confuse the two is normal. In Santa Fe and around northern New Mexico, they are farolitos. In places where luminaria bonfires are uncommon, farolitos are called luminarias. But whatever they are called, the glow from the lovely little lanterns definitely means Christmas in the American Southwest.

Framed by the warm glow of farolitos, carolers gather around a blazing luminaria to sing in celebration of the season.

Taos Pueblo, New Mexico, shown here with a season-fitting dusting of snow, is home to the Church of San Geronimo, where parishioners celebrate the Virgin Mary on Christmas Eve and Christmas Day.

La Buena Noche

Christmas Eve, the good night, has come. Friends and family who "seek shelter at the inn" are welcomed in to be warmed with food, song, and laughter. Guests are served hot chocolate with bizcochitos and buñuelos, or a full Christmas dinner. Holiday food is plentiful and offered at every opportunity during Christmas in a Hispanic home.

When family and friends sit down for Christmas Eve dinner, the meal is a combination of traditional Mexican and Native American foods. There must be *tamales*—filled with meat and spices, traditionally wrapped in corn husks and steamed—and *posole*, a stew of hominy, combined with pork, red chile, and onions or some other variation. There are *enchiladas*, *menudo* (tripe stew), plenty of chile sauce, Indian bread, *empañaditas* (rich pastry turnovers), and *capirotada*, a delicious cinnamon-flavored bread pudding filled with cheese, piñon nuts, and raisins.

Warmed by the company and the food, it is time to bundle up and head outside for a walk through the neighborhood or a trip downtown to see the Christmas Eve *luminarias* and the *farolitos*.

La Misa de Gallo

The evening grows late. Soon it will be time to head for church and *La Misa de Gallo*, the Mass of the Rooster, the Midnight Mass named after a Christmas legend.

According to Mexican folklore, the animals in the stable were distressed that no one other than Mary and Joseph was there to witness the birth of the Christ Child. Taking charge of the situation, a rooster flew to a high perch and announced the good news. Soon, other roosters took up the cry, spreading the word about the coming of the Messiah.

In Santa Fe and other small towns, the late night walk home from church affords one last chance to admire the many rows of little lights and to visit while warming up at the occasional luminaria.

For many families, Christmas dinner, the festive *comida de Navidad*, follows Midnight Mass and stretches through the late-night hours. Two more Christmas Day services follow, at dawn and at noon, and many people attend all three.

Christmas in the Pueblo

Christmas Eve and Christmas Day at the pueblos are filled with dancing, prayer, and religious processions. Blazing luminaria bonfires are lighted at sunset on Christmas Eve on the pueblo square and before the mission church. The fires honor the Christ Child and welcome worshipers.

Inside the Church of San Geronimo at Taos Pueblo in New Mexico, parishioners begin a night of hymns and prayers. In the midst of vespers, a group of young men walk outside the church, line up, and fire rifles into the cold night air. Later, a procession from the church travels around the village's ancient plaza, carrying the statue of the Virgin Mary. Accompanying Mary is an order guard of Taos men in ceremonial dress, who carry rifles that they periodically fire into the air. The gunshots are fired to protect the Virgin Mary as she is paraded around and to chase away evil spirits.

Southwest Christmas Past

What was Christmas like for the first homesteaders and ranchers in the Southwest? It was make do and make merry. Arriving from back East or from across the Atlantic, newcomers found able replacements for any Christmas supplies their new homes lacked.

Wherever evergreens grew, there were traditional Christmas trees of pine or spruce. Southwest piñon pines, chopped up to build luminaria bonfires, soon found a place inside homes, festooned with decorations. In sandy, scrub brush regions where no plant looked like a traditional tree, resourceful settlers made trees Southwest style.

Ever-rolling tumbleweeds, gathered and stacked three together, made plump, bushy "trees" ready to decorate. Wrapped with strings of popcorn, frosted raisins, and cranberries, plus homemade decorations of paper flowers and dyed cotton balls, only someone with a sharp eye could tell what was really underneath. A small mesquite, with its twisty branches, thorns, and all, could hold a host of delicate blown-glass ornaments that had been carefully packed and carried from Germany to Texas.

German immigrants settling in the American Southwest brought their Christmas customs with them. Those customs have become a lasting part of this region's celebration of Christmas.

Tumbleweeds have long been used to decorate the Christmas season in the Southwest. Here they have been crafted into figures for a truly unique nativity scene in Rancho de Chimayo, New Mexico.

To decorate mantels and tabletops, settlers collected branches of juniper and yaupon, a native holly with shiny green leaves and red berries, and arranged them with pine cones and fruit.

When the railroad made its way into the region in the 1870's, fancy manufactured Christmas ornaments quickly replaced homemade decorations. With glittering tinsel and magical blown-glass creations from Germany now easy to acquire, Christmas trees soon found their place in almost every home, and the home decorations grew more ornate.

CHRISTMAS FOR CHILDREN

On Christmas Eve, the children would search their drawers for just the right stocking to hang. In bigger, better style, many little Texans would hang a pair of stockings, knotted or pinned together at the top, from a nail in the fireplace mantel. For lack of a mantel, the stocking would be draped over the back of a child's chair or bed footboard.

Like children everywhere, ranchers' and homesteaders' children in the 1800's and early 1900's would find fruit, nuts, hard candies, and small toys in their stockings. But there also were likely to be firecrackers, sparklers, and sky rockets stuffed along with the treats. Christmas Day always ended with a bang as the children, farmers, ranch hands, and cowboys lit up their own pieces of the Southwestern sky.

Christmas presents ranged from homemade dolls to real guns. For children living on isolated ranches or in the scattered tiny towns where schools were too poor to provide supplies, books were prized Christmas gifts. According to one old Southwestern custom, a child who was quick to shout "Christmas gift!" upon meeting a friend or stranger on Christmas Day was entitled to a present from this person. It is not clear how often presents actually were won in this way, but the tradition of calling "Christmas gift!" continues to this day in some communities, with or without material reward.

OLD TRADITIONS IN A NEW LAND

Christmas was a time for settlers in a rugged new land to relax in the familiar comforts of age-old holiday traditions. Today Christmas in the Southwest is a rich blend of the traditions and tastes various immigrant groups brought with them from "the old country."

German Christmas trees and memories

German customs, which are a charming part of Christmas in Texas, trace their history back to a nobleman's plan. Between 1845 and 1847, some 7,380 German immigrants arrived in Texas, sponsored by the German *Adelsverein,* or Association of Noblemen.

Schoolchildren of St. Patrick's Mission in Anadarko, Oklahoma Territory, in 1906 clutch their dolls and other gifts as they gather around the Christmas tree.

The heritage doll is a popular Christmas gift for children of today's Southwest. Found at the Pastores Feed and General Store of Los Ojos, New Mexico, these dolls are really two dolls in one. On one end they are clearly Native American, but turn it upside down and a new doll of definite Hispanic descent is revealed.

Believing that Germany had become overpopulated, this organization's backers encouraged Germans to start up a colony of their own in Texas's open territories.

The plan also seemed like a way to make money. The noblemen bought, sight unseen, a tract of dry and barren land miles northwest of Austin, expecting the property to immediately improve with the arrival of German settlers. The newly titled owners were not told that the Comanche were in control of "their" property.

Luckily, led by Prince Carl of Solms-Braunfels, the immigrants never traveled that far. Instead, the prince, who had a vision of ruling in this new world, purchased land along the Comal River, and the city of New Braunfels was born. Later a second group of Germans bought another site, also far from the unpromising promised land, and named it Fredericksburg after Prince Frederick of Prussia. These two "way station" towns remain to this day German strongholds in Texas, and they are wonderful places to enjoy German traditions, Texas style.

In New Braunfels, the Sophienburg Museum sits on the hilltop where Prince Carl built a log fortress named Sophienburg (Sophie's Hill, in honor of his wife). The museum joins other German-heritage organizations in town to host a traditional *Weihnachtsmarkt,* which kicks off the Christmas celebration in November. At the three-day Christmas market, Texans can feast on German holiday foods, shop for handmade Christmas decorations and craft items, and enjoy German beer, wine, and Wassail, the traditional Christmas hot cider. "Cowboy Kringle," a happily Texanized German fellow, is always on hand for the fun.

St. Nicholas followed the German settlers to Texas. Just as he had in the old country, the kindly old man leaves special treats for children in New Braunfels, Fredericksburg, and all over Texas on his special day, December 12. Then, on Christmas Eve, little descendents of the German settlers eagerly await the arrival of Kris Kringle, a messenger from the Christ Child, who brings presents to be opened that night.

The Christmas tree, also a German immigrant, received a warm welcome in the Southwest. Finding none of the fir trees they associated with Christmas in their homeland, German settlers trimmed native junipers and pines for the holidays. Today the tradition of decorating junipers and pines continues.

San Antonio, where German immigrants helped build a

The restored Steves Homestead of San Antonio, Texas, is a stately symbol of the town's proud German heritage. The public is invited to tour the mansion during the Christmas season.

beautiful city, also has its share of imported traditions. One of the stately restored German houses in the King William District of San Antonio is the Steves Homestead, home of Ed Steves, a German cabinetmaker who arrived in San Antonio in 1848 to become one of the city's most successful businessmen. During Christmas, the San Antonio Conservation Society welcomes the public to tour the Steves mansion, which is decorated for the holidays in keeping with its German-Victorian heritage. A German-style holiday market in November helps open the holiday season in San Antonio.

Zweite Weihnachten, meaning "Second Christmas," is a German celebration that found a second home in the American Southwest. Taking place on December 26, Zweite Weihnachten in the Southwest was traditionally a day for visiting friends and making Christmas merry with dances, games, and maybe a firecracker or two. Today the custom still provides a great reason for getting together in New Braunfels, Phoenix, and many other places across the Southwest where German settlers made their homes.

Czech immigrants made their mark on Christmas in the American Southwest with unique foods, dances, and music. The Tex-Czech Christmas season begins with the Feast of St. Nicholas on December 6.

Tex-Czech Christmas

In the second half of the 1800's, Texas became home to a number of Czech immigrants whose Christmas customs enrich the lives of Southwesterners everywhere.

Throughout the Southwest, Christmas is a great excuse to eat *kolacky,* the irresistible Czech Christmas pastry loved by all. It would not be Christmas here without the little melt-in-your-mouth folded star with a rich fruit center.

Czech immigrants also supplied music for the Christmas dance. Everyone down here celebrates by dancing, and whether it is a polka, Texas swing, Tex-Mex, or Cajun music, the accordion—brought to Texas by Czech immigrants—is an essential part of the Southwestern sound.

In Czech farming communities in central and eastern Texas, the Christmas celebration begins with the Feast of St. Nicholas on December 6. Czech tradition holds that St. Nicholas descends from heaven on a golden rope. He is accompanied by an angel who records the good and bad deeds of children and a devil who menaces children with a whip and rattles a chain to warn them to improve their behavior.

Texas stars and Polish star men

Texas claims the first Polish settlement in the United States, the town of Panna Maria, founded in 1854. Seeking a new home and religious freedom, Father Leopold Moczygemba and 100 Polish families landed in Galveston in late fall 1854. They walked 200 miles to the junction of the San Antonio River and the Cibolo Creek. Arriving on Christmas Eve, the new Texans named their settlement *Panna Maria* (Virgin Mary) and quickly set about building a church.

Panna Maria established the first Polish school in the United States, and Polish remained the first language of Texans in that area. Other Polish communities, with names such as Cestohowa, Pawelkville, and Kosciusko grew from this first settlement. And so, too, did Polish Christmas traditions.

When the first evening star, symbolizing the Star of Bethlehem, appears in the Christmas Eve sky, Polish families come together for a Christmas feast filled with symbols and meaning. By custom, there must be an odd number of dishes served, an even number of diners, and an empty place set for the Christ Child. *Oplatki,* white wafers symbolizing the Sacred Host, are presented with the meal. The food itself represents a hope for a bountiful harvest in the year ahead.

Before heading off to Midnight Mass, children of the house receive a visit from Star Man, who asks them religious questions and passes out small gifts. He is accompanied by Star Boys, dressed as nativity figures ranging from Wise Men to sheep.

Norse myth and merriment

Several groups of Norwegian settlers made their way to central Texas in the mid-1800's. With them came more Christmas magic.

The Norsemen taught Texans how to "shoot in Christmas" (see Chapter 3). And they gave them an excuse to keep mistletoe around all year. It was the Norse notion that mistletoe would protect a house from burning down. At Christmas, these settlers also would ward off bad luck by burning a "Yule candle" from dusk till dawn.

The annual Lutefisk Festival, which descendents of these Norse settlers put on early in December in Cranfills Gap, Texas, adds a delicious, steaming hot dish to the Southwestern Christmas feast. Hundreds of bales of *lutefisk* (codfish steeped in lye) are imported each year to be carefully prepared following complicated traditional methods, then served to 1,000 or more people in the local school cafeteria. Lutefisk covered with boiled white potatoes, melted butter, and white sauce and served steaming hot tastes like Christmas to those in central Texas.

Scandinavian Christmas Fun

An influx of Scandinavian settlers in the late 1800's added other charming Christmas customs to the Southwestern mix.

By tradition the Scandinavian Santa, an elf named *Jultomten,* makes the rounds on Christmas Eve wearing a red cape and riding in a sleigh pulled not by reindeer, but by a goat. *Julbock,* the "Christmas goat," has become a popular symbol of the season in Texas and throughout the Southwest. Straw Julbocks are a common sight at Southwest Christmas craft fairs.

The Scandinavian *julklapp,* or Christmas box, also has added fun to the season in the Southwest. By custom, the gift giver leaves a mystery gift, then knocks or rings the bell and runs to hide before being discovered. The gift itself may be wrapped in strange wrapping or in boxes within boxes. Some gift givers leave only a clue, sending the receiver on a hunt for the julklapp.

Fort Concho in San Angelo, Texas, is the country's best preserved fort from the Indian War era (1866–1891). The fort played an important part in the settlement of the Southwest and offers a historical Christmas celebration during its "Christmas at Old Ft. Concho" event in December.

STEPPING BACK IN TIME

Taking great pride in their past, the descendents of early homesteaders, shopkeepers, ranchers, cowboys, and all the rest merrily join in a terrific assortment of "Christmas Past" living-history events staged throughout the Southwest each December.

Jourdan-Bachman Pioneer Farm Christmas

What was Christmas like on a Southwestern homestead farm in the 1880's? On a tenant farm? On a commercial cotton farm? At the northeast edge of Austin, Texas, period-dress volunteers are busy tending to the cattle, chores, mending, and baking, so they can "ready up" things and demonstrate.

On three evenings in mid-December, the Jourdan-Bachman Pioneer Farm, a full-time reenactment of a 75-acre 1880's farming community, welcomes modern folks to take a candlelight tour of the Christmas their ancestors cherished.

Taking a hayride around a large cornfield, visitors first arrive at the tenant farm, once the home of a recently freed African American family. Here a cozy group pops corn over the fire, tells stories, and simply enjoys the comfort of their own company by candle- and firelight. Stopping next at the log cabin of first-generation homestead farmers, visitors are treated to Christmas carols of the 1800's and Victorian Christmas trimmings, plus a sampling of Christmas cooking from the period. At the commercial cotton farm, a band plays lively music from the 1880's, and folk dance lessons are ready for all who want to join the fun. And at the farm's dairy barn, children can learn how to write with a quill pen or make a tussie-mussie. There are free cookies, too.

Christmas at Old Fort Concho

The country's best preserved fort from the Indian War Era (1866-1891), Ft. Concho in San Angelo, Texas, provides for a wonderful weekend-long frontier fort Christmas.

Founded in 1867 to protect stagecoaches and wagon trains and escort the U.S. mail, Ft. Concho played an important part in the settlement of the southwest and southern Great Plains. A number of infantry and cavalry units were stationed at the fort, including all four regiments of the Buffalo Soldiers, the African American fighting forces.

Now a national historic landmark, each year the fort fills its 23 original and restored buildings and 40-acre site with the sights, sounds, and tastes of December in the late 1800's for its "Christmas at Old Ft. Concho" event.

Visitors can partake in a cowboy campfire breakfast, watch period military drills or cavalry and artillery demonstrations, listen to string bands and marching bands, dance, enjoy the wit and wisdom of cowboy poets and storytellers, "make and take" all kinds of old-fashioned Christmas decorations, and sample traditional Christmas fare.

Along with a modern artisan, craft, and food fair, the event features a "Post Traders" fair where shoppers can browse an 1800's tent city, encountering period-dress traders with a variety of replica goods to sell.

A Territorial Christmas celebration

For one month, between Thanksgiving and Christmas, the town of Guthrie, Oklahoma, returns to its Victorian-era heyday, rough edges and all, in a Territorial Christmas celebration.

It was in the Victorian age that the Christmas celebration hit its stride in England and the United States. Guthrie came to life then, too. As capital of the Oklahoma Territory, Guthrie was the center of railroad, banking, and cultural life for a large region. A beautiful old town filled with Victorian architectural treasures (and the nation's largest contiguous historic district), Guthrie celebrates the season in an all-town, month-long, back-to-the-past Christmas party set sometime between 1890 and 1910.

Guthrie, the first town in Oklahoma to have electricity, strings tiny white lights all over its lovely old downtown buildings and trims every edge with evergreen garlands, lace, and ribbon. Period carolers and peanut vendors stroll the sidewalks, while carriages and surreys drive by. Restaurants and the town's many bed-and-breakfast hotels feature holiday foods of the era. There are candlelight trolley tours and nightly performances by bell choirs, barbershop quartets, church choirs, and bluegrass bands. A highlight of the

Christmas lights help define the Victorian architecture that is characteristic of the town of Guthrie, Oklahoma. This beautiful old town celebrates its heritage at Christmastime each year.

month-long event is the Territorial Ball, where period dress is optional.

A certain rascally charm is added to the festivities by the honesty of the town's look back. During the Victorian era, Guthrie was a pretty—and pretty rough—place, housing 14 or 15 bordellos. The Reeves brothers, owners of the wildest saloon in the Oklahoma Territory, were prominent Guthrie citizens. Tough as they might have been all year long, the Reeves boys always provided free Christmas dinner and drinks for all. One of the brothers was known to hand out money freely to anyone who asked for help around the holidays.

There is no doubt that the traditions of the native peoples of the American Southwest, together with those of the many immigrants to the area, have transformed Christmas Past into a Christmas Present that Southwesterners will cherish for many a Christmas Future.

Dickens on The Strand

The stately Victorian iron-fronted buildings were here waiting for people to return—and they did, bringing a Dickens of a Christmas celebration with them.

"Dickens on The Strand" participants dressed in attire fitting of a Dickens story stroll the streets of the The Strand National Historic District of Galveston, Texas, during the elaborate annual Christmas event.

In the 1800's, when Galveston carried on a lively cotton trade with England, The Strand Street and surrounding district was "the Wall Street of the Southwest." Each year this historic district near the waterfront comes to life as Galveston gathers for its annual "Dickens on The Strand" Christmas extravaganza.

District streets illuminated by gaslights and lanterns are filled with characters straight from a Dickens story—a town crier, street urchins, fine ladies, rakish young men, and British bobbies. Even Bob Cratchit with Tiny Tim or a disheveled ghost of Jacob Marley may make an appearance.

More than 6,000 people stroll the streets and work the shops, dressed in Victorian garb. Another 50,000 to 90,000 "regular folks" attend the weekend festival.

"Dickens on The Strand" has given the former financial district a Christmas present of new life. When the first Strand celebration was held nearly 25 years ago, the district was down and out. The buildings were empty and in poor repair, and the streets were deserted. To highlight the possibilities of Christmas Future, supporters held the first Strand event under cover of night. Vacant buildings were skillfully decorated and lit with lanterns. The district's former charm glowed brightly; its shabby state faded in the shadows.

From that first lantern of hope, The Strand District has grown stronger with each year's Christmas celebration. Today The Strand National Historic District bustles with life all through the year. Proceeds from The Strand's holiday event have helped to restore 17 blocks of the district to Victorian standards.

CANDLELIGHT AT OLD CITY PARK

Situated at the edge of downtown Dallas, Old City Park is a 13-acre living-history museum that includes 35 restored historic structures, ranging from a log cabin to the largest

The gazebo of Old City Park in Dallas is decorated to reflect the the traditions of Christmases past. The park is host to a number of events that celebrate the season in the "old-fashioned way."

surviving antebellum mansion in the city. On the first and second weekends of December, the museum holds a special candlelight event to celebrate the wonders of Christmases past.

In addition to the traditional Christmas decorations of "Anglo" settlers, various buildings reflect the African American, Spanish, and Jewish celebrations of the season.

Between stops inside the buildings, each richly decorated in the style of its time, visitors are entertained by carolers, bell choirs, and spirited 1800's reenactments. Storytellers and hands-on craft activities help bring the past to life for children.

To round out the experience, there are old-fashioned holiday gifts on sale at McCall's General Store, plus plenty of traditional baked goods to sample.

The wide-open ranches of the Southwest are a beautiful backdrop for the celebration of Christmas. And no one can rope in Christmas like a cowboy can.

Cowboy Christmas

For ranchers and cowboys, the Southwest was full of possibility. There were vast farmlands and wide-open cattle ranges. Ranches were big; towns were small and far apart. A fella could do well for himself—and he could get a little lonely.

To let a person go on feeling lonely just did not seem right around these parts. In the past, the grand ranches of west Texas threw open their doors at Christmas, bringing ranchers, cowboys, and townspeople from miles around together for rollicking Christmas dances. And that gracious attitude continues today.

Early celebrations

In the early days of Texas, a Colonel and Mrs. Goodnight welcomed as many as 175 guests from across the west Texas panhandle to feast at long tables laden with roast beef, wild turkey, antelope, and all kinds of cakes, pies, and Christmas sweets. Each year, the Nussbaum brothers of west Texas held a "protracted" Christmas dance at their White Deer Ranch. Cowboys and local girls danced till early morning to the music of a big-city orchestra, breaking only to refresh their energy and their spirits at lavishly spread tables.

Dances, at the White Deer Ranch or at a neighbor's home, were the social event loved by all in early Texas and Oklahoma. In true Southwest style, everyone was welcome, everyone had a dance partner, and even the shyest girl or most awkward fellow was pulled out onto the floor. These folks knew a thing or two about loneliness, and they were not about to cause it for anyone.

Christmas today

Christmas on the Texas Panhandle today continues to be a triumph for Christmas cheer. Folks are few and far between, but they know how to find Christmas together in Cimarron County, Oklahoma.

Kenton, the westernmost town in Cimarron County, the westernmost part of the Oklahoma Panhandle, is small by any standard, with a population of 42. Still, Kenton—located 6 miles from the Colorado border, 2 miles from the New Mexico border, 28 miles from Texas, and 50 miles from Kansas—can draw a crowd for Christmas. Each year more than 200 long-distance neighbors gather at an old, wooden-floored, four-room former schoolhouse in Kenton for an "old-timey" Christmas party.

Like the early settlers before them, these panhandlers still know how to make their own fun. At the Kenton party, children dressed in their Christmas best recite poems or sing solos. There is a string band, a piano player, caroling, plenty of Christmas fare, a piñon tree strung with popcorn, and loads of Christmas cheer. Even Santa Claus finds his way to the old school with a sack of treats in tow. And there is always a surprise in store: a Christmas poem written by a local cowboy, a nativity scene with cardboard animals and local Wise Men, or maybe a choir singing "Home on the Range" to fiddle accompaniment.

The Cowboys' Christmas Ball

In 1885, M. G. Rhodes, the proprietor of the Morning Star Hotel in Anson, Texas, a tiny cow town of two dozen inhabitants, had a wonderful idea. He circulated word from one

A couple dressed in period garb waltzes after the Grand March of the Cowboys' Christmas Ball at Pioneer Hall in Anson, Texas.

cow camp to the next about "great doings" at the Morning Star. He decorated the hotel with mistletoe and Christmas trimmings; hired a caller to direct dances; and brought in fiddle, tambourine, and banjo players to set a lively pace. He did all this in the name of the first Cowboys' Christmas Ball.

Ladies and cowhands, delighted at the invitation, rode in from isolated farms and ranches dressed to a tee to dance the square, Virginia reel, schottische, and heel-and-toe polka. A much-loved annual tradition was born. When, in its second or third year, the Christmas ball was held in honor of a popular cowhand's marriage, that became a lasting part of the fun. Newlywed couples were chosen to lead off the dancing ever after.

Today the Cowboys' Christmas Ball draws celebrants from everywhere in Texas and beyond. The Morning Star Hotel is gone—lost to a fire—but a new stone Pioneer Hall, built in 1934 for this specific purpose, welcomes a capacity crowd of 850 to Anson's three-day Cowboys' Christmas Ball reenactment on the weekend before Christmas.

Modern cowboys squire ladies wearing period dresses of the 1880's about the floor. The couples dance squares and reels and, these days, plenty of Texas two-steps. Newlywed couples still are invited to lead the opening march. With more than 1,000 requests for tickets, some sent a year in advance, the Texas Cowboys' Christmas Ball Association members wonder if they should build a bigger hall.

Poetry, singin', and pictures

For cowboys who are likely to feel a poem coming on at Christmas, Wickenburg, Arizona, presents its annual Cowboy Christmas get-together, a weekend of "poetry, singin', and pictures."

On the first weekend in December, cowboy and cowgirl poets—and folks just hankerin' to hear some good western verse and storytelling—gather at the Desert Caballeros Western Museum in Wickenburg. Some cowboys sing their verse while others recite against a changing backdrop of western scenery. With ribbons to win and fun to be had, as many as

Folks gather at Christmastime to share western-style poetry, singin', and pictures at the Desert Caballeros Western Museum in Wickenburg, Arizona.

30 poets and a crowd of 1,500 have gathered at the Cowboy Christmas event that gets bigger and better every year.

Before the Saturday morning poetry performances, there is a traditional cookout breakfast with plenty of hot coffee and biscuits. Between readings, cowboys and cowgirls tour the museum's western exhibits or take in a "ranch album" video. Late Saturday night, cowboy storytellers compete with rousing renditions of "real" experiences on the range during the Wild Cow Tales Contest. Sunday morning, the Cowboy Christmas conference closes with a ranch-style outdoor worship service.

SHOOTING IN CHRISTMAS

While plenty of old-time cowboys had poetry in their hearts, they also had guns in their holsters. Christmas cheer on the

Gene Autry: Christmas Cowboy

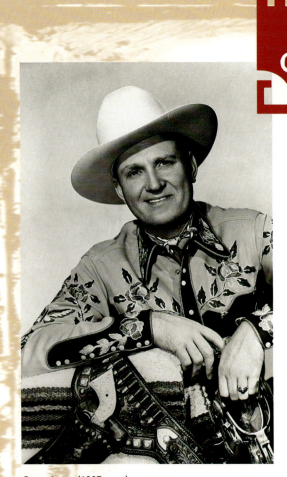

Gene Autry (1907—   )

With his 1949 hit recording of "Rudolph the Red-Nosed Reindeer," Gene Autry roped Christmas and cowboys together forever.

Born in Tioga Springs, Texas, in 1907, Autry worked on his uncle's ranch in Oklahoma before a stint on the radio in Tulsa launched his career as America's favorite singing cowboy. Then came Christmas. The 1947 classic, "Here Comes Santa Claus," which Autry co-wrote and sang, became a platinum seller and part of every child's personal repertoire. Next Autry recorded "Rudolph," which sold 25 million copies—more than any other Christmas song except "White Christmas." In 1950, he followed this hit with "Frosty the Snowman." In all, this lanky gentleman cowboy with his white Stetson hat and big Texas grin starred in nearly 100 films. He wrote or co-wrote more than 200 songs and recorded 635, earning the 1991 Lifetime Achievement Award from the Songwriters Hall of Fame.

How cowboy was Christmas for Autry? Witness "The Night Before Christmas, In Texas That Is" from the album *Gene Autry's Christmas Favorites* (CBS, Inc.).

range was *loud*. Many guns were fired in celebration, and fireworks, homemade or imported, were as traditional as carols.

Norwegian settlers who came to central Texas in the mid-1800's are credited—maybe blamed—with introducing a Christmas custom that rowdy cowboys quickly took to heart. Ancient Norse superstition held that witches wandered the countryside on Christmas Eve. To chase off lurking evil spirits, young men would creep up outside houses and shoot their guns.

If they wanted to aim at something, shooters in the old Southwest could join in a Christmas hunt or shooting contest. They still can. In Raton, New Mexico, and in places throughout the Southwest, traditional hunting and shooting contests are an annual holiday tradition.

The Night Before Christmas, In Texas That Is

'Twas the night before Christmas in Texas, you know,
Way out on the prairie, without any snow.

Asleep in their cabin were Buddy and Sue,
A'dreamin' of Christmas, like me and you.

Not stockings, but boots at the foot of their bed,
For this was in Texas, what more need be said.

When all of a sudden from out the still night,
There came such a ruckus it gave me a fright.

And I saw 'cross the prairie like a shot from a gun,
A loaded up buckboard come out at a run.

The driver was geein' and hawin' with will,
And horses, not reindeer, he drove with such skill.

C'mon, Buck and Poncho, and Prince to the right,
There'll be plenty travelin' for you all tonight.

The driver, in Levis and a shirt that was red,
Had a 10-gallon Stetson on top of his head.

As he stepped from his buckboard he was really a sight,
A beard and a moustache so curly and white.

As he burst in the cabin, the children awoke,
And were both so astonished that neither one spoke.

And he filled up their boots with such presents galore
That neither could think of a single thing more.

When Buddy recovered the use of his jaws,
He asked in a whisper, "Are you Santa Claus?"

"Am I the real Santa? Well, what do you think?"
And he smiled as he gave a mysterious wink.

Then he leaped in the buckboard and said in his drawl,
"To the children of Texas, Merry Christmas, you all!"

"The Night Before Christmas, In Texas That Is"
Words and Music by Leon Harris Jr. and Bob Miller
© Copyright 1951 MCA MUSIC PUBLISHING, A DIVISION OF MCA INC. Copyright Renewed.
ALL RIGHTS RESERVED.   INTERNATIONAL COPYRIGHT SECURED.   USED BY PERMISSION.

Lighting the Western Sky

The stars shine big and bright over the American Southwest. And so do Christmas lights. Everywhere, dazzling displays of electric bulbs fill the dark December sky with holiday cheer as Southwesterners string their homes, businesses, and towns with lights of many colors.

Fantasy of Lights

The citizens of Tempe light up their town in style during an amazing three-month extravaganza. They drape downtown Tempe alone in more than 100,000 lights. Then they stage a seemingly endless party.

Statistics tell the Tempe festival story: 8,523 miles of lights outline 65 downtown buildings. More than 500,000 people attend the 222 official events. During the opening

More than 100,000 lights illuminate downtown Tempe during the town's Festival of Lights Christmas celebration.

At Honor Heights Park in Muskogee, Oklahoma, tiny bulbs depict wildlife and outline the park's natural beauty as part of its "Garden of Lights" Christmas celebration.

ceremonies, a fireworks display explodes every 4.83 seconds. Finally, in a city where the average December daytime temperature is 73.4° F, 10 tons of real snow are dumped for snowball throwing and snowman building during the festival's "Snow Daze" event.

As part of the festival, the Kris Kringle Market—in the style of the traditional Bavarian lighted outdoor marketplace—presents the handiwork of local artisans. Next door to Tempe, the Phoenix Desert Botanical Gardens hosts its beautiful traditional lights display, "Noches de las Luminarias," and the Phoenix Zoo adds to the fun with "Zoo Lights!" every night during the Christmas season.

Natural Christmas beauty

Each year, thousands drive or stroll through Honor Heights Park in Muskogee, Oklahoma, to view the 120-acre park's lovely azalea bushes in bloom. Now they are coming in much greater numbers to see the park's Christmastime "Garden of Lights."

This light show is a natural wonder. There are no lighted candy canes, elves, or snowmen. Rather, the park's bushes flower with lights everywhere. Lights also wrap tree branches and outline a 200-foot waterfall, celebrating the park's natural beauty. The only lighted figures are deer, squirrels, rabbits, and children—all beings that are natural to the park. In lights overhead, three graceful white doves seem to fly across the park, magically decorating it as they pass.

In the park's Five Civilized Tribes Museum, visitors find handcrafted ornaments and holiday gift items created by local Native American artists who use only natural materials.

Red Rock Fantasy

With spectacular Christmas light displays set against the towering beauty of Sedona, Arizona's red rocks, fantasy seems the perfect name. From Thanksgiving until mid-January, Los Abrigados, a 22-acre village-style resort set along a creek surrounded by majestic red rock canyon walls, lights up Christmas with its Red Rock Fantasy.

The resort presents more than 60 glittering light displays, featuring Southwestern, religious, traditional, and famous-character themes. During the holiday season, the public is welcome to stroll through the resort and take in the 1-million-lights show, then stop for a chestnut roast, take a horse-drawn wagon ride, meet Santa, listen to old-fashioned carolers, or visit the resort's oversized gingerbread house. Visitors are free to simply linger and look or to top off the evening with a holiday toast or dinner at Los Abrigados.

Volunteer Spirit Shines Bright

In Oklahoma, the Chickasha Festival of Lights is a sight to see: 1.5 million tiny lights set Chickasha's Shanoan Springs Park sparkling. Here visitors find lighted

Ornaments and holiday gift items crafted by Native American artists reveal the beauty of combining native traditions with modern Christmas customs.

dancers floating on a lake; the Three Wise Men; and Santa galloping on horseback. Another 1.5 million lights shine throughout five neighborhoods surrounding the park. It is hard to miss the park thanks to "America's Tallest Christmas Tree," a 16-story structure strung in 20,000 lights during the holidays, which remains standing throughout the year.

Named 1995 Oklahoma Event of the Year, the Chickasha Festival of Lights is also a top tour recommendation of the American Bus Association. No wonder. Shanoan Springs Park's light-drenched "Crystal Bridge" alone is worth the trip.

Even more impressive than its award-winning Christmas lights display is the mighty volunteer effort that puts Chickasha in lights. More than 800 townspeople turn out to

Symbolically lighting the way to Bethlehem, San Antonio's Paseo del Rio, or River Walk, is a breathtaking sight at Christmas.

turn on the lights. Senior citizens check the bulbs, teenagers build scaffolding, and residents have raised $90,000 to support the Christmas display. And Chickasha's Christmas cheer is long lasting. The town's residents are proud to say that they are now using that same teamwork to do other things for their community throughout the year.

Fiesta de las Luminarias

On weekend evenings just before Christmas, San Antonio places thousands of glowing luminarias along its beautiful downtown Paseo del Rio, or River Walk. The lights symbolically light the way for the Holy Family's journey to Bethlehem. Added to the 50,000 tiny blue, red, and green lights hanging from the pecan, cypress, and magnolia trees overhead, the little rows of candles in paper sacks present a breathtaking display.

Every evening between Thanksgiving and Christmas, carolers cruise the River Walk, filling the air with holiday cheer. More than 185 school, church, and company choral groups take part in the holiday boat caroling event. The River Walk holiday celebration opens with a lighting ceremony and riverboat parade in late November. Santa himself arrives with the parade, riding on a flower-strewn barge.

Decorating the holiday season with lights has become a tradition for all who celebrate Christmas. For many, the lights represent the star that led the Wise Men to the stable in Bethlehem where Jesus was born. And in an effort to symbolize this reminder of the true meaning of Christmas, Southwesterners light up their portion of the earth in their own unique style. Like the Star of Bethlehem, the lights of the American Southwest guide the way for those who want to celebrate Christmas Southwestern style.

River of lights

In the early evening dark of a late December night, the southern Rio Grande River near Sunland Park, New Mexico,

Local artist George Gonzalez sets a farolito afloat on the Rio Grande River near Sunland Park, New Mexico. Gonzalez began the Christmastime tradition of setting the river aglow more than 10 years ago.

sparkles with a simple, and simply amazing, celebration of Christmas.

Following a tradition started by local artist George Gonzalez, a volunteer army of children and adults from Sunland Park sets free in the river a farolito flotilla of thousands of lighted votive candles wrapped in tiny handmade foil floats. Resting against the many sandbars that dot the river in winter or slowly moving along with the shallow river's current, the more than 4,000 glowing, twinkling lights are a magical sight.

Every bit as moving is the volunteer effort behind the glowing river display. The river candles were first launched more than 10 years ago by Gonzalez as a gesture of thanks for the blessings in his life. Devotion to the display quickly spread. Today a host of volunteers collect candles throughout the year and make the boats in preparation for the last Saturday night before Christmas.

The star of the Lone Star State

El Paso's Star on the Mountain first twinkled on a Christmastime night in 1940. Today the big, bright star shines out every night of the year over Texas's "Star City."

The El Paso Electric Company put that first small star on the south side of Franklin Mountain overlooking El Paso. Trouble was, it was only 50 feet wide, and its red bulbs barely could be seen from the highway below. Then it seemed as though the end had come when the star's lights quickly blew out in a storm.

But the Star on the Mountain had charmed the city of El Paso. Soon a bigger, better star was in the works. By 1946, a star 459 feet long and 278 feet wide made of 459 white bulbs—the same as today's star—was ready for Christmas.

From its lofty position near the mountaintop, the star can be seen from the east for 100 miles from the air and 30 miles from the ground. Like a real star, the El Paso star is used by pilots as a navigation point. Since World War II, it has been lighted every Christmas. The star also remained lit all through the Iran hostage crisis and later throughout the Gulf War in support of American troops. In recent years, the star is lighted every night from 6 p.m. until midnight, sending out a Christmas message of hope all through the year.

Oh, Christmas derrick, Oh, Christmas derrick

Kilgore, Texas, is proud of its past as an oil boom town, and that pride shines bright at Christmas.

In 1930 this little city sat at the center of the East Texas oil rush. Back then, more than 1,200 oil derricks stood within the Kilgore city limits. Entrepreneurs even drilled through the floor of the Kilgore National Bank in search of oil.

Today the three tall derricks, which remain at the center of town—strung with lights and wearing a "Merry Christmas" banner and a star on top—stand as Kilgore's community Christmas tree. On every downtown street corner, and on many corners throughout Kilgore's neighborhoods, six-foot metal derrick replicas are being permanently positioned as a citywide salute to the past. Each corner derrick wears a star at Christmas.

"The World's Richest Acre," a city-block-sized section of Kilgore that hosted two dozen working wells during Kilgore's heyday, is now preserved as a park. Here, too, bright Christmas lights bring a festive glow to the oil well works.

Big City and Small Town Celebrations

They looked at the barren desert vistas with their ragged mesquite trees and piñon pine, at the rocky canyons and open plains, at the wide, starry sky, and they saw Christmas. With the perfect setting at hand and Christmas in their hearts, Southwesterners quickly began creating Bethlehems of their own.

The City of Bethlehem

A beloved tradition was born in Madrid, New Mexico, in 1927. The once-booming mining community was floundering. Work was slowing at the mine and spirits were low when a group of miners decided to bring Christmas to life.

What started with a few people and a few lights, within a few years had grown into an all-town celebration. Moved to a nearby canyon, Madrid's Christmas display became a life-sized, realistic depiction of the life of Christ. A visit to Madrid's Bethlehem became an annual Christmas pilgrimage for people from many miles around.

By 1947, the failed mine had left Madrid a near ghost town. Still, New Mexico's Bethlehem was alive with

From the smallest pueblo to the largest city, citizens of the Southwest celebrate a Christmas that rejoices in the diversity of their cultures. Here, Santa Claus joins in a Christmas Day buffalo dance in the San Ildefonso Pueblo of New Mexico.

Christmas spirit—in a new home. The newly formed Lions Club of Ratón, New Mexico, a small town in the Sangre de Cristo Mountains, took up the Madrid tradition. With the support of the entire town and cooperation from local businesses, the Ratón Lions Club gave the tradition a proud new life.

Located in Climax Canyon at the edge of town, Ratón's "City of Bethlehem" presents an outdoor lighted sequence of the events surrounding the birth of Christ. For nearly 50 years, thousands of people have traversed from afar to pass by the trumpeting angel at the city's gate and follow the circular drive through the canyon, viewing scores of scenes from the Christmas story as they listen to Christmas music.

In 1983, Madrid, which has been reborn as an artists' enclave, revived its Christmas tradition. Now on the first and second weekends in December, the town hosts a holiday open house. Beginning at the end of November, the town lights up much as it did in the 1930's. More than 6,000 lights, along with an artificial tree atop a mountain south of town, are illuminated every evening into early January.

Children get in the act

Possibly the most charming Christmas reenactment is the Living Christmas Pageant presented by the children of Boys Ranch Town, a Baptist home for children in Edmond, Oklahoma. For three nights on the first weekend in December, visitors can drive through the ranch to view 10 scenes from the life of Christ and listen to a taped narration. Children at the ranch create the settings, and they bring the scenes to life.

The Boys Ranch pageant, a tradition for more than two decades, draws large crowds of visitors and is eagerly anticipated by the children at the ranch each year. Pageant fun is spreading through the state, with other Baptist children's homes now staging performances of their own.

The Wonderland Express

Chugging more than 40,000 actual miles—that is 2,000,000 scale miles to the trains—around and through the tracks in their delightful tiny world, the Galleria Wonderland Express locomotives haul all kinds of happiness to Texas children every Christmas.

Texas's largest holiday train exhibit features 23 locomotives and more than 400 cars laid out in a 6,500-plus-square-foot retail space in Dallas's Galleria shopping center. The trains speed over a realistically detailed route, traveling from the

Rocky Mountains to the city of Dallas, steaming across open plains, through small country towns, under bridges, through tunnels, and alongside towering pine trees. For the delight of visitors, charming surprises await. For example, at the drive-in theater the classic "It's a Wonderful Life" is playing. Heart-warming details such as this are always being added, which keeps this a "must-see" tradition year after year. Each child's visit also cheers another child, as proceeds from the Wonderland Express benefit the Ronald McDonald House of Dallas, a charitable foundation that provides support for critically ill children and their families. Open from mid-November through the first week in January, the Galleria Wonderland Express trains are enjoyed by more than 100,000 visitors each year. In their first seven years of service, the trains have raised more than $1.5 million.

A Christmas apple festival

There are apples, apple cider, apple pie, apple cobbler, and more apples—the more the merrier for a Christmas celebration in Willcox, Arizona. On the first weekend in December, this southeast Arizona town invites the world to the annual Willcox Christmas Apple Festival.

Willcox residents stage a Christmas parade and tree lighting, an arts and crafts fair, a cooking-with-apples contest, and a holiday bazaar. Apples are everywhere—apples to eat, to put on your tree, to hang from your ears. There are apples carved from wood and apples crocheted onto pillows.

The apples are harvested in early fall, so why an apple festival at Christmas? Apples are all red and green and shiny like Christmas decorations. And, well, "It's a great excuse to have a party," confess the townsfolk. In Willcox, apples are cause for celebration. When the grain market failed years ago, local farmers found the soil, sun, and underground water—combined with the chill of a 4,100-foot elevation—perfect for growing all kinds of apples. And what apples they are! All that sun gives a Willcox apple a sugar content two to four percent higher than any other apple in the world.

Angels descend from on high before onlookers to the "City of Bethlehem" display in the New Mexico town of Ratón. The display, which is located in Climax Canyon, is the town's premier event at Christmastime.

Phantom Ranch, tucked away at the bottom of the Grand Canyon, offers a unique, meditative Christmas getaway.

A Grand Canyon Christmas

The Grand Canyon, one of the most spectacular canyons in the world, cuts right through northwestern Arizona in Grand Canyon National Park. The canyon extends 277 miles and is 1 mile deep. By anyone's standard, the Grand Canyon is a majestic sight. It seems almost obvious that Christmas here would be very special indeed.

At the Shrine of Ages, an interfaith religious center at the edge of the pine forest and only a few hundred yards from the Grand Canyon's rim, hundreds of candles glow in celebration each Christmas Eve. About 350 people gather for the interdenominational candlelight service held early on Christmas Eve. There are park rangers and their families, people from the nearby Grand Canyon Village, and people who come from all over the West and all over the world to be here on this night. The Shrine's floor-to-ceiling window brings the beauty of the Canyon close as worshipers hear the Christmas story, hold candles, and sing carols. A second, smaller service follows at 11:30 p.m., for people seeking a quiet, meditative Christmas moment.

To reach Phantom Ranch, visitors must ride mules down a twisting trail that drops more than a mile in elevation.

Phantom Ranch, which sits where three trails meet along a clear, cold stream at the bottom of the Grand Canyon, is booked months in advance for Christmas Eve. All 92 rental beds, every cabin, and every space in the bunkhouses is taken. Visitors come from all over, making reservations as early as a year in advance, to spend Christmas in this unique getaway. To reach the ranch, lodgers must ride mules or walk down a twisting trail that drops more than a mile in elevation. The ranch boasts no gaily trimmed tree, no pile of presents, no grand Christmas dinner; just a commune with the Canyon.

Why do visitors come here from around the world, Christmas after Christmas? Some say it is to get away from the commercial trappings of Christmas. Others talk about renewal and reflection. For all, it is a chance to feel the spirit of Christmas while surrounded by the overwhelming beauty of the Grand Canyon.

Worshipers to the Shrine of Ages, an interfaith religious center located just yards from the Canyon's rim, gather for an interdenominational candlelight service on Christmas Eve.

The glorious "Messiah"

Tulsa residents claim that their city hosts the ultimate performance of George Frideric Handel's oratorio *Messiah*. And with good reason. For 75 years, the First Lutheran Church of Tulsa has been staging a *Messiah* that grows more complex and inspiring each year.

Since its first presentation in 1921, the church has never missed a Christmas *Messiah*. Even when the bass singers were overseas during World War II, parts were reworked for women's voices, and the performance went on. In the 1950's, the Tulsa church began inviting other area choirs to join their production.

Today voices from 16 area Lutheran churches come together in one 170-member choir, supported by a 20-piece orchestra. Breathtaking antique glass slides depicting the life of Christ are projected overhead during the performance. The beautiful music is interspersed with Scripture readings and accompanied by a costumed Christmas pageant.

Deck the trees

In cities all over the Southwest, a Festival of Trees, featuring Christmas trees decorated according to various traditions, is a lovely part of the Christmas celebration.

The Philbrook Museum of Art in Tulsa turns up the charm during its Festival of Trees event. The trees, sponsored by local businesses and designed by area artists, range from the beautiful to the beautifully bizarre. There might be a tree constructed completely of computer monitors, a recycled products tree, or a "tree" of reindeer antlers strung all over with Christmas lights. The museum also presents specialty ornaments handcrafted by famous designers. In addition to the trees and ornaments, more than 125 gingerbread creations, handcrafted by schoolchildren and some of Tulsa's finest chefs and bakers, make up a gingerbread village as part of the festival.

Also in Oklahoma, at the Kirkpatrick Center Museum in Oklahoma City, visitors can walk through "a brilliant forest of trees," also known as Holiday Treefest: An International Celebration. Each of the 40 trees on display reflects a specific international theme and is adorned with at least 900 lights and 350 ornaments. Holiday Treefest takes place from late November until January 1. And while the trees take center stage, numerous special events entice visitors of all ages.

The First Lutheran Church of Tulsa, Oklahoma, stages a spectacular production of George Frideric Handel's oratorio "Messiah" every year at Christmastime.

Serving up Christmas

Early settlers in the Southwest knew lean Christmases and made do without as they homesteaded on the rugged plains or traveled the rough trail west. They survived by depending on one another. Though ranches and farms were few and far between, neighbor helping neighbor became their way of life.

Today that Southwestern neighborly spirit lives on, shining a bright welcoming light at Christmastime. Whether inviting in friends and family or reaching out to a stranger in the street, Southwest doors open wide to share Christmas cheer. A heartwarming example of this spirit comes in the form of the Red Andrews Christmas Dinner. Fifty-five years ago, Oklahoma boxing and wrestling promoter Ernest "Red" Andrews took a look at the poor boys parking cars for his events at the old Stockyard Coliseum in Oklahoma City. He decided he could make a difference in their lives. Red put on a Christmas dinner to bring cheer to needy families in Oklahoma City. Every Christmas Day since, the Red Andrews Christmas Dinner has been providing plenty for all who want to come.

By 5:30 a.m. on Christmas Day, volunteers are already on

hand, offering steaming cups of coffee to those waiting in line for the Red Andrews Christmas Dinner. By day's end, 6,000 to 7,000 people will have dined on turkey and all the trimmings. Heading home, they carry bags stuffed with oranges, apples, and for the children, new toys and a picture taken with Santa.

Though Andrews died 20 years ago, his family and scores of contributors and volunteers keep up the good work in his name. Dinner guests come from all walks of life, and no one is turned away.

Christmas on Parade

Across the Southwest, everyone is on parade at Christmas. From the world-famous Adolphus/Children's Parade in Dallas to marches through the tiniest towns, parades are an essential part of Christmas in every corner of the Southwest.

"For children only"

The eyes of Texas—and of people the world around—turn to Commerce Street in Dallas on the first Saturday in December to see Christmas come to town with the Adolphus/Children's Christmas Parade. The only Christmas parade designated "for children only," thousands in Dallas

Mickey Mouse waves to onlookers as he floats down Commerce Street in Dallas's Adolphus/Children's Parade.

attend the event and watch on television around the world.

Every float and character in the Adolphus/Children's Christmas Parade is designed with children in mind. Storybook and movie "stars" such as Mickey Mouse, Batman, Barbie and Ken, and Cookie Monster can be found on Commerce Street during the parade.

Started nearly 10 years ago as a gift to the children of Dallas from the Adolphus Hotel, the parade is now sponsored by Neiman-Marcus and the Children's Medical Center of Dallas. Proceeds from the sponsorship of floats, giant inflatables, and marching bands all benefit the medical center.

The Adolphus/Children's Parade would not be complete without the arrival of Santa Claus riding on his sleigh.

A visit from Santa

In Arizona, Santa makes his first visit each year on the weekend before Thanksgiving at the Winslow Christmas parade. People from miles around turn out to cheer the annual Christmas parade.

The small-town charm of Winslow's celebration is hard to resist. There is a house-decorating contest, a high-school band contest, and a tree-lighting contest for which each school makes its own decorations. As many as 120 parade entries register each year. Sitting at the edge of "Indian country," Winslow also prominently features Native American performances in its Christmas event.

Parading down Main Street

In the friendly town of Woodward, Oklahoma, they never miss an opportunity to march down Main Street. Woodward, which also hosts the more than 60-year-old Elks Rodeo Parade, throws itself into a Santa-centered Christmas parade.

When the parade reaches its midtown destination, everyone, carrying candles and song sheets, walks to Santa's house to sing carols. Woodward tradition dictates that all the children jingle little bells until Santa rides up on his Harley.

All the Trimmings

Celebrating Christmas just feels right in the American Southwest. Holiday taste treats, trimmings, and traditions old and new simply abound here.

The Collin Street Bakery

Even those who insist they do not like fruitcake cannot help but indulge in the Collin Street Bakery Original Deluxe. This Texas treasure of a fruitcake has been gobbled up year after year by celebrities and common folk alike. The most popular fruitcake in the world, the Original Deluxe was even enjoyed in outer space by the Apollo astronauts.

This much-loved Christmas taste tradition was born in 1896 when German master chef, and immigrant Texan, August Weidmann improved an old German fruitcake recipe by adding native Texas hard-shell pecans. One hundred Christmases later, orders for Weidmann's Collin Street Bakery Original Deluxe pour in from around the world.

A jolly snowman greets shoppers in Taos, New Mexico, as they prepare for their Southwestern Christmas holiday.

August Weidmann (with vest) stands outside his Collin Street Bakery in the small town of Corsicana, Texas, in 1910 (right). Today, the Collin Street bakers still create the Original Deluxe fruitcake, touted as the most popular cake of its kind in the world.

Since the shy Weidmann and his business partner Tom McElwee, a flamboyant Texas entrepreneur, opened the Collin Street Bakery in the tiny town of Corsicana, Texas, the company has never missed a Christmas. Still a small family business, operated today by the McNutt family, the Bakery produces approximately 4 million pounds of fruitcake per year, filling more than 1.5 million orders every holiday season.

The secret of the fruitcake's success lies first in its unique recipe, featuring pecans as the largest single ingredient, equaling 27 percent, by weight, of each cake. Other ingredients include locally harvested, pure clover honey; pineapple and papaya from the company's own plantations; white raisins from southern California; and cherries from the Midwest and Northwest.

Still, even a great-tasting product needs to be taste-tested. Tom McElwee had established a luxury hotel above the original bakery. When famous travelers stopped at the hotel, McElwee would hide a fruitcake in their luggage. As soon as they reached home, former guests were writing back for more. A big break came when McElwee's friend John Ringling and his circus troupe came through town. The fruitcakes left in their luggage traveled the rest of the tour through the United States and Europe. Orders started pouring in from everywhere, and the top-performing mail-order business in the world was born.

Pecans aplenty

When Christmas came to the Southwest, indigenous American hard-shell pecans were scattered everywhere. The Native Americans who first walked these lands found groves and groves of majestic pecan trees lining the river valleys of Texas and Oklahoma. Along rivers such as the Guadalupe in Texas (called the "River of Nuts" in the native language), the area's early inhabitants scooped up pecans by the handfuls and made these nutritious nuts a staple of their winter diet.

Pecans get their English name from the Algonquin word *pakan*, meaning "nuts so hard they require a stone for cracking." These tasty nuts are well worth the extra effort. Native peoples ate pecans whole, pounded them into meal, used pecan oil for cooking, boiled pecan tree sap to make syrup, drew dyes from the pecan hull, even created a fish poison from the pecan husk, then burned the trees as firewood.

The state tree of Texas, the native pecan is a proud American. Pecan trees line most of the rivers in Oklahoma and Texas. In Oklahoma, they are grown in 62 of the state's 77 counties. Today, the state of Georgia is the largest producer of pecans in the world. Texas ranks second, producing 60 million pounds of pecans. New Mexico follows with a 30-million-pound crop, and Oklahoma, where pecans are the number one fruit or nut crop, ranks fourth with a 20-million-pound crop. Arizona, a smaller producer, is itself home to the largest single pecan farm, a spread of more than 6,000 acres.

Southwest native pecans are sold at every grocery store in the country and all around the world. But the best-tasting pecans are sold at country roadside stands in Texas and Oklahoma. What a treat: Pecans carried home fresh from the trees to be shelled and stirred into a Christmas pie!

Mistletoe country

Mistletoe grows wild, very wild, across Texas, Oklahoma, New Mexico, and Arizona. Texas claims to provide 95 percent of the mistletoe needed to meet the United State's yearly Christmas-kiss requirements. Oklahoma has designated mistletoe as its official state floral emblem.

Mistletoe is native to the American Southwest. Most of the United States's Christmastime supply of this white-berried plant comes from this part of the country.

Still, you won't find a Society of Mistletoe Growers anywhere down here. In fact, Southwestern landowners spend more time chopping down mistletoe than encouraging it to grow. Mistletoe is a weed that attaches itself to a host tree, then survives by leeching energy from the tree. Over time, mistletoe can weaken or even kill its host tree.

Yet to see mistletoe purely as a pest is to overlook not only the power of a kiss, but also mistletoe's essential role in the yearly food cycle for some of the world's most beautiful creatures.

America's migrating songbirds arrive in Arizona, Oklahoma, and Texas in time for Christmas. And once here they find a rich supply of plump, nutritious mistletoe berries. Mistletoe provides birds with a reliable food source, while its bushy greenery offers protection from the elements. Returning the favor, birds carry tiny mistletoe seeds on their beaks from tree to tree.

Bloomin' poinsettias

Texas played a key role in making the poinsettia plant a Christmas tradition. During the Christmas season in 1828, Dr. Joel R. Poinsett, the first U.S. ambassador to Mexico, was

A Christmas tree made of poinsettia plants in full bloom stands majestic in the atrium of the state capitol building in Oklahoma City, Oklahoma.

south of the border negotiating to buy the territory of Texas for the United States. Poinsett, a botanist, was entranced by the brilliant red leaves of the plant the Aztecs called *cuitlaxochitz* ("false flower") and the Mexicans called the "Flower of the Holy Night." The diplomat brought home cuttings for his greenhouse in South Carolina and sold cuttings to a nursery in Philadelphia.

Soon the brilliant red plants, renamed in Poinsett's honor, were in demand at Christmas all across the country. Today Texas ranks in the top 10 producers of poinsettias.

Southwest traditions spread

Bright red dried chile peppers—home-grown Southwest decorations—are quickly becoming hot holiday items everywhere. Woven into wreaths, hung in traditional chile *ristras*, or strung around the tree as electric chile lights, these well-known symbols of the Southwest are finding their way into homes across the country at Christmas and all through the year.

And another Southwest tradition, luminarias, has made its way into Christmases in other parts of the United States. For many years, the brown paper sacks with candles inside gave a soft, magical glow to homes, churches, and walkways only in the Southwest. Now Christmas shops across the country stock luminarias—plain or in Christmas colors and some with punched-out designs. For safer decorations, there are even strings of electric luminarias.

Ristras of bright red dried chile peppers have become a traditional Christmas decoration in the American Southwest, and their charm is quickly spreading to other regions of the United States.

The Neiman Marcus Christmas Book

First issued in 1915 as a Christmas card inviting shoppers to the Dallas store for holiday shopping, the *Neiman Marcus Christmas Book* is eagerly anticipated each year by a following of more than 3 million serious shoppers and window shoppers around the world.

Neiman Marcus sprinkles among its catalog pages exclusive offers of his-and-hers airplanes; real Egyptian mummy cases; and a 14-karat gold train set with a gold and diamond engine hauling four carloads of loose rubies, sapphires, emeralds, and diamonds.

After its introduction in 1915, the catalog did not appear again until 1926, and then it was only 16 pages. But those pages were filled with unusual, humorous, and beautiful gifts—each one a Neiman Marcus exclusive. A tradition was born.

In the 1950's, brothers Stanley and Edward Marcus kicked the unusual gift notion into high gear with the offering of a Black Angus steer, on the hoof or in steaks, complete with a silver-plated outdoor cooker. The public loved the idea, and the challenge was set. The next year, the first "His and Hers" gifts debuted—a pair of Beechcraft airplanes. Since then, the *Neiman Marcus Christmas Book* has never failed to delight and surprise.

Indeed the trademarks of Christmas in the American Southwest are so delightful that they will continue to influence the celebration of Christmas everywhere for many years to come.

Anything goes when it comes to Christmas decorations in the Southwest. As a case in point, these cacti have been decorated as the Three Wise Men.

SOUTHWEST CRAFTS

POINSETTIA PLACEMAT

This placemat makes a colorful addition to any holiday table.

WHAT TO DO*

1 Using tracing paper and pencil, trace the large oval shown on pages 66-67. The oval should be 15 inches wide and 10 inches tall. Trace the two poinsettia leaves and one of the circles shown on page 66.

2 Cut the oval, leaves, and circle shapes out of the tracing paper to make your patterns.

3 Place the oval pattern on the green felt. Using a felt-tip pen, trace around the shape. Remove pattern. Cut the oval shape out of the felt.

* If you need help, ask an adult to lend a hand.

MATERIALS*

- tracing paper
- pencil
- felt-tip pen
- scissors
- red and green felt, ¼ yard of each
- small piece of yellow felt
- craft glue

* Makes one placemat

4 Place the large leaf pattern on the red felt. Using the felt-tip pen, trace around the shape. Remove pattern. Cut the leaf shape out of the felt. Repeat this step until you have 16 large leaves.

5 Place the small leaf pattern on the red felt. Using the felt-tip pen, trace around the shape. Remove pattern. Cut the leaf shape out of the felt. Repeat this step until you have 6 small leaves.

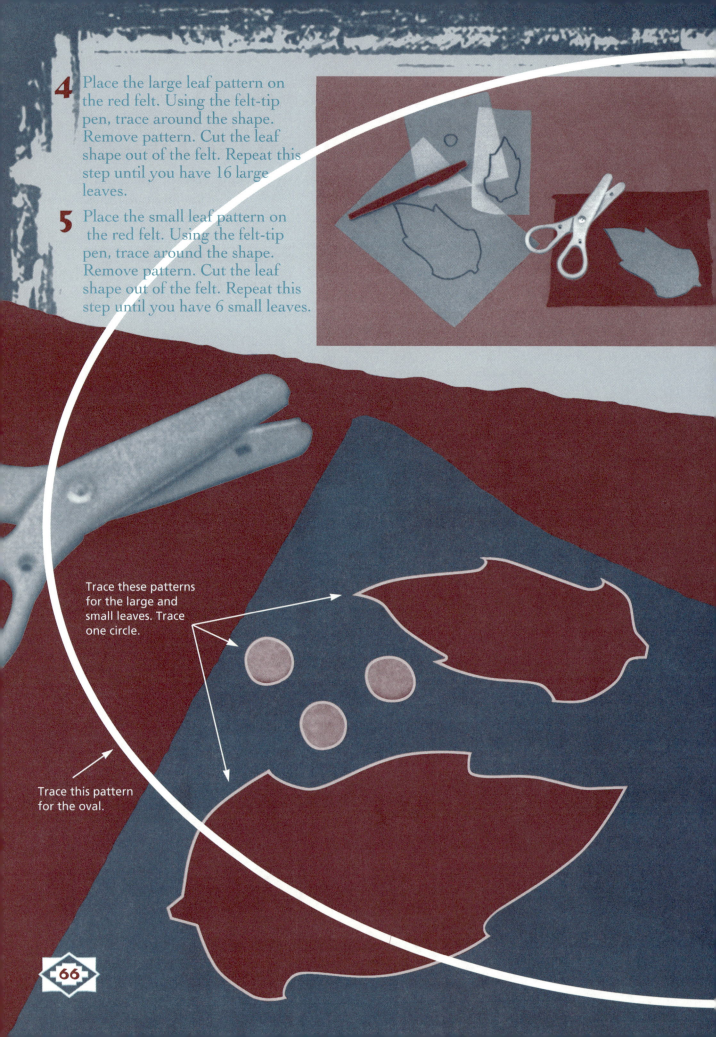

Trace these patterns for the large and small leaves. Trace one circle.

Trace this pattern for the oval.

6 Trace the circle pattern and cut it out of the yellow felt. Repeat this step until you have 6 circles.

7 Now you can start to assemble your placemat. First, place the green oval on a flat surface. (When placing all shapes, be sure the side you traced on is facing down so that the tracing marks will not be seen on the finished placemat.)

8 Arrange 10 of the large red leaves in a circle on the green oval. The tips of the leaves should be either touching or overlapping the edge of the oval. The leaves can overlap each other to fit around the oval.

9 After the leaves have been placed, glue them in position by placing craft glue on the underside of each leaf and pressing down.

10 Arrange the 6 remaining large red leaves on top of the first layer. This layer should be closer in to the center of the oval, again overlapping each leaf to fit the shape. Once you have spaced out the leaves, apply craft glue to the undersides and press down.

11 To make the third layer, arrange the 6 small leaves around the center of the oval, overlapping to fit. Once you have spaced out the leaves, apply craft glue to the undersides and press down.

12 To finish your placemat, arrange the 6 yellow circles in the center of the flower and glue them in place.

13 Allow your placemat to dry completely before you use it to decorate your holiday table.

Sponge Painting

These sponge stamps can be used to decorate cards, gift tags, or wrapping paper.

Materials
- tracing paper
- pencil
- felt-tip pen
- scissors
- package of sponges; each sponge should be no more than ½-inch thick
- objects to decorate, such as drawing paper, blank cards, clay pots, cardboard boxes
- poster paints
- shallow bowls
- paper towels

What to Do*

1. Using tracing paper and a pencil, trace the four shapes shown here. If you want, you can also design your own patterns. Carefully cut out the patterns.

2. Place one of the patterns on a sponge, and trace around it with the felt-tip pen. (If sponge is much larger than pattern, trim it a little before tracing.)

3. Carefully cut out the shape.

*If you need help, ask an adult to lend a hand.

4 Pour a small amount of paint into a shallow bowl. Paint should form a thin layer on the bottom of the bowl.

(You will need a separate bowl for each paint color.)

5 Dip one side of the sponge into the paint. Be sure the entire flat surface of the sponge is covered.

6 Blot the sponge on a paper towel once or twice to remove any excess paint.

7 Press the sponge down on what you're decorating, and lift it off carefully. Repeat this step to make a pattern, rewetting the sponge in the paint when needed. (You can do this 3 or 4 times before you have to add more paint.) You might want to practice a few times on some scrap paper to get a feel for how hard to press.

(If you want to use the same sponge pattern for more than one color, wash and dry the sponge before using it for another color.)

8 Allow your sponge painting to dry completely. Drying times may differ, depending on the object. A clay pot will take longer to dry than paper.

Clay Ornaments

Hang these ornaments on your tree or wreath, or decorate gift packages with them.

Materials

- tracing paper
- pencil
- scissors
- air-drying clay*
- rolling pin or dowel rod
- craft knife
- househould objects such as a paintbrush, fork, paper clips
- paints
- drinking straw
- ribbon

*available at arts and crafts stores

What to Do*

1. Trace the ornaments shown on pages 70 and 71 using tracing paper. Carefully cut out the patterns. Ask an adult for help if needed.

2. Role out a slab of clay a little larger than your pattern. Clay should be about ¼-inch thick.

3. Place the pattern on the clay and carefully cut around the pattern with a craft knife.

4. You can add texture to your ornament by using household items to make indentations in the clay. For example, you can use a pencil point to draw an eye and a scarf for the coyote. Or you could use the end of a thin paint brush to make the lines on the cactus. You might want to experiment with other household items like paper clips or the prongs of a fork to add different textures.

*If you need help, ask an adult to lend a hand.

5 While the ornament is still laying flat, make a hole for a ribbon hanger by poking a drinking straw near the top of the ornament. The clay should come up in the straw and leave a clean hole.

6 Let the ornament dry thoroughly according to the directions on the package.

7 To further decorate the ornament, paint it after it has dried.

8 To finish the ornament, make a ribbon hanger for it by cutting a 12-inch piece of ribbon. Thread it through the hole in your ornament. Leaving a large loop, tie a bow at the top. Now your ornament is ready to hang.

Adobe Candle House

This farolito makes a lovely gift— for yourself or a friend!

Materials*

- paper
- pencil
- ruler
- scissors
- air-drying clay*
- rolling pin or dowel rod
- craft knife
- decorating objects such as paper clip, paintbrush, toothpick
- paints
- votive candle in glass holder

*available at arts and crafts stores

What to Do*

1. Using tracing paper, trace the pattern of the flattened candle house on pages 72-73. Include the door and the windows in your tracing.

2. Cut the windows and door out of your traced pattern.

3. Role out a slab of clay to fit your pattern. Clay should be about ¼-inch thick.

4. Place the pattern on top of the clay slab. Cut the clay along the pattern edge. Using the edge of a ruler will help you cut smoother top and bottom edges.

5. Cut out holes for the windows.

6. The door can be left attached, or you can cut down one side and across the top so door will be partly opened on the finished house.

7. Decorate your house by adding textured designs to the clay. You can use many different kinds of objects to make designs, such as a pencil, ruler, paper clip, toothpick, or the end of a paintbrush.

* If you need help, ask an adult to lend a hand.

8 Carefully lift the clay slab and shape it into a circle. Overlap the ends to close the circle, and press the ends together.

9 Let the clay dry, following the directions on the package.

10 You can use paint to further decorate the house.

11 Have an adult insert a votive candle inside the adobe house and light it for you. (The candle should be in a glass holder.) Display on a tabletop or other flat surface away from curtains and where it cannot be knocked over.

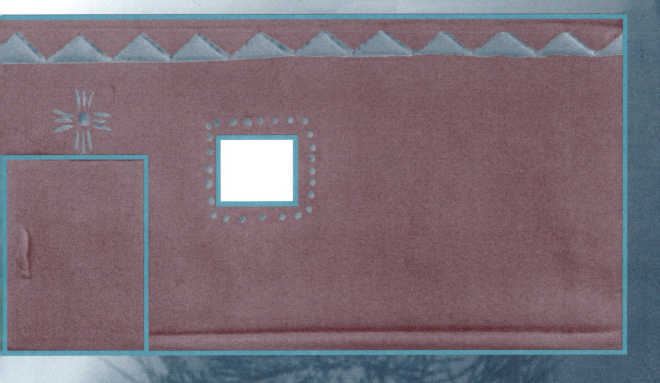

Southwest Carols

Cradle Song

Oh sleep, thou Holy Baby— with Thy head against my breast; Meanwhile the pangs of my sorrow are soothed and put to rest. A la ru— a la me— A la ru— a la me— A la ru— a la me— A la ru- a la ru- a la me

Thou need'st not fear King Herod,
He will bring no harm to you;
So rest in the arms of Your mother
Who sings you a la ru.

A la ru, a la me,
A la ru, a la me,
A la ru, a la me,
A la ru, a la ru, a la me.

From Royal Jerusalem

From Mount Tabor came Saint Gabriel,
Where he long had been abiding,
And to Bethlehem in Jewry
He did go, the shepherds guiding.
And to Bethlehem in Jewry
He did go, the shepherds guiding.

Come, oh shepherds, come rejoicing,
Come and bring your hermit brother
To adore the Holy Infant
And to praise His sovereign Father.
To adore the Holy Infant
And to praise His sovereign Father.

Come, oh shepherds, come defying
The anxiety which holds you,
To adore the Holy Infant,
Though the bitter cold enfolds you.
To adore the Holy Infant,
Though the bitter cold enfolds you.

And their royal gifts displaying,
Come the Kings unto the manger,
God their hearts will keep from danger
Who are thus His laws obeying.
God their hearts will keep from danger
Who are thus His laws obeying.

Southwest Recipes

Southwest Black Bean Soup

12 oz. dried black turtle beans*

8 cups chicken or vegetable stock

2 tbsp. olive oil

1 whole onion, chopped

1 cup chopped celery

1 cup chopped carrots

2 cloves garlic, minced

2 tsp. dried oregano

1 tsp. dried thyme

1 bay leaf

½ tsp. cayenne pepper

3 tbsp. fresh lime juice

sprigs of fresh cilantro for garnish (optional)

Rinse and sort turtle beans, discarding any that are shriveled or discolored. Place beans in a large stockpot. Cover with water and soak overnight in refrigerator. Drain beans and return to stockpot. Add chicken or vegetable stock and heat to boiling. Meanwhile, in large skillet, heat olive oil over medium-high heat. Add onion, carrot, celery, and garlic, and sauté until vegetables are crisp-tender. Add to stockpot along with oregano, thyme, bay leaf, and cayenne pepper. Reduce heat and simmer, covered, for 3 to 4 hours. Transfer soup to blender or food processor, and pureé to desired thickness. Just before serving, add lime juice. Garnish with fresh cilantro (optional). Add salt and pepper to taste. Makes 8 servings.

* commonly called black beans

Kathryn's Southwest Salsa

5 to 6 medium tomatoes, peeled

1 medium onion, coarsely chopped

2 cloves garlic, minced

1 tsp. olive oil

1 tsp. sugar

2 fresh green chiles, diced, or 1 small can green chiles, drained

juice of 1 lime

2 tbsp. fresh cilantro, chopped

Place tomatoes in pot of boiling water for approximately 30 seconds. Remove with slotted spoon. When slightly cool, remove skin. In bowl of food processor, place tomatoes, onion, garlic, olive oil, sugar, green chiles, lime juice, and fresh cilantro. Process with on/off switch until mix is coarsely chopped. Add salt and pepper to taste. Serve with tortilla chips as an appetizer, or with grilled poultry. Makes approximately 2 cups.

SOPAIPILLAS

4 cups all-purpose flour

1 tsp. baking powder

½ tsp. salt

2 tsp. sugar

1½ tsp. corn oil

¼ cup evaporated milk, room temperature

½ cup lukewarm water

oil for deep frying (canola or corn), to a depth of 2 inches

honey

Sift together the flour, baking powder, salt, and sugar in a large mixing bowl. In a separate small bowl, mix together corn oil, milk, and warm water, and pour all at once into the dry ingredients. Using your hands, work the dough until a sticky ball forms.

Lightly dust a pastry board or counter with flour, and knead the dough for approximately one minute. (The dough will be soft but not sticky.) Cover dough with a cloth and allow to rest for 15 minutes. Divide the dough into three parts, and cover once again and allow to rest for 30 minutes.

Roll out each ball of dough on lightly floured surface to ¼-inch thick. With a sharp knife, cut each circle of dough into four wedges and cover with damp cloth. Do not stack wedges, as they may stick together.

In a deep skillet or wok, heat the oil to 400°. (If the oil smokes before reaching the desired temperature, it cannot be used for this recipe. Select a different type of oil. Try to use fresh, high-quality oil.) Gently drop each dough wedge into oil. When top surface has fully puffed, turn the sopaipilla over with tongs, being extremely cautious. Cook until light golden and remove with tongs. Drain on paper towels. Repeat with remaining wedges. Drain sopaipillas on paper towels and arrange in a cloth-lined basket. Serve immediately with honey. Makes 24 sopaipillas.

CALABACITAS

2 tbsp. olive or corn oil

1 medium onion, chopped

1 clove garlic, minced

1 lb. medium zucchini, sliced

1 12-oz. can corn, drained

½ cup chopped green chiles

½ cup grated cheddar or Monterey Jack cheese

salt and freshly ground pepper to taste

Sauté onion, garlic, and zucchini in the oil until onion is translucent. Mix in corn and green chiles; cover and heat thoroughly. Just before serving, mix in cheese. Add salt and pepper to taste. Makes 4 servings.

Margarita Chicken

4 boneless, skinless chicken breasts

½ cup tequila

¼ cup olive oil

¼ cup fresh lime juice

¼ cup fresh orange juice

2 garlic cloves, minced

½ tsp. salt

⅛ tsp. freshly ground pepper

8 lime wedges for garnish (optional)

Gently flatten chicken breasts with the palm of your hand. In a large bowl, combine tequila, olive oil, lime juice, orange juice, garlic, salt, and pepper. Add chicken breasts and marinate for up to 2 hours at room temperature, or overnight in the refrigerator. Bring to room temperature before cooking.

Preheat broiler or barbecue grill. Drain chicken and arrange in shallow baking pan, or place on grill. Cook 7 to 8 minutes per side, or until done. Arrange chicken breasts on platter and garnish with lime wedges, if desired. Makes 4 servings.

Grilled Marinated Pork Tenderloin

1 cup freshly squeezed
    orange juice

6 tbsp. soy sauce

¼ cup olive oil

2 tbsp. chopped fresh
    rosemary, or 2 tsp.
    crumbled rosemary

3 cloves garlic, minced

dash of Tabasco™ sauce

freshly ground pepper

2 12-oz. pork tenderloins

Combine first seven ingredients in a medium bowl. Add pork tenderloins and marinate in refrigerator overnight, or at room temperature for one hour.

Preheat oven to 400°. Drain pork, reserving marinade. Place pork on baking sheet and roast until cooked through, about 30 minutes. Conversely, preheat barbecue grill and place pork on grill. Cook until done, approximately 30 minutes.

Meanwhile, bring marinade to a boil in a small saucepan. Slice pork tenderloins and serve, passing sauce separately. Makes 6 servings.

PINEAPPLE AND JICAMA SALAD

1 fresh pineapple (approximately 2½ pounds), peeled, cored, and cut into chunks

1 large jicama, peeled and cut into 2-x-½-inch matchsticks

1 pound seedless red or green grapes, halved lengthwise

¾ cup fresh basil, finely chopped

½ cup safflower oil

⅓ cup fresh lime juice

1 tbsp. sugar

¼ tsp. salt

freshly ground pepper

½ pound red leaf lettuce

In a large bowl, toss together the pineapple, jicama, grapes, and basil. In a small bowl, whisk together the oil, lime juice, sugar, salt, and pepper. Pour half the dressing over the fruit and toss well. Refrigerate for up to two hours.

In a large bowl, toss the leaf lettuce with the remaining dressing. Arrange the lettuce leaves around the edges of a platter and mound the pineapple-jicama salad in the center. Makes 6 to 8 servings.

TEXAS PECAN PIE

½ cup butter or margarine

¾ cup light brown sugar

3 eggs, slightly beaten

1 cup dark Karo™ syrup

¼ tsp. salt

1 tsp. vanilla extract

2 cups coarsely chopped pecans

1 unbaked pie shell

whipped cream (optional)

Preheat oven to 350°. In a large bowl, cream together the butter and brown sugar until fluffy. Add the eggs and beat until the mixture is smooth. Mix in the syrup, salt, and vanilla extract. Spread the chopped pecans in the bottom of the unbaked pie shell and pour the egg mixture over them. Bake the pie at 350° for 40 to 45 minutes, or until a knife inserted in the filling comes out clean. Cool on a rack for at least one hour. Can be served with whipped cream, if desired. Makes 6 to 8 servings.

ACKNOWLEDGMENTS

COVER	Gene Peach
2	Tom Bean, DRK
6	Edward McCain; Stephen Trimble
7	Dick Canby, DRK
8	Terry Shoulders
11	Russell Bamert
12	Don B. Stevenson
14	Russell Bamert
15	Joel Salcido
16	Randall Roberts
17	Gene Peach
18	Geraint O. Smith
20	Sophienburg Archives
22	Randall Roberts
23	Sue Smith; Oklahoma Historical Society
25	Jim Argo
26	Duke Petree, U.S. 7th Infantry Living History Unit
28	Fort Concho Museum
30	Jim Argo
31	Art Meripol, ©*Southern Living*
32	Old City Park, Dallas
34	David Stoecklei, AdStock Photos
36	Sandra Chittum
37	Wickenburg Chamber of Commerce
38	Corbis-Bettmann
40	Scott Mitchell, Tempe AZ Tourism
42	Howard Robson; Oklahoma Tourism

43	Russell Bamert
44	Bob Daemmrich
46	Joel Salcido
49	Stephen Trimble
51	Tom Wagers
52–53	Fred Griffin
55	Howard Robson
56–57	The Adolphus/Children's Christmas Parade
59	Terry Shoulders
60	Collin Street Bakery
61	Gary R. Zohn, DRK
62	Fred Marvel, Oklahoma Tourism
63	Gene Peach
64	Don B. Stevenson

CRAFT PHOTOGRAPHY:
Joann Seastrom*

ADVENT CALENDAR FRONT:
Russell Bamert

ADVENT CALENDAR WINDOW ILLUSTRATIONS:
Carol Brozman*

RECIPE CARDS:
WORLD BOOK photos by Dale DeBolt*

MUSIC:
Todd Smith*

All entries marked with an asterisk (*) denote illustrations created exclusively for World Book, Inc.